PHONICS

Vic's Fish and Chips

Written by
Sue Graves

Illustrated by
Mike Phillips

Practising phonemes of more than one letter
and simple polysyllabic words
+ and / the / to / go / he / she

First published in 2009 by
Franklin Watts
338 Euston Road
London NW1 3BH

Franklin Watts Australia
Hachette Children's Books
Level 17/207 Kent Street
Sydney NSW 2000

Text © Sue Graves 2009
Illustration © Mike Phillips 2009

A CIP catalogue record for this book
is available from the British Library.

ISBN: 978 0 7496 9153 0 (hbk)
ISBN: 978 0 7496 9162 2 (pbk)

Series Editor: Jackie Hamley
Series Advisors: Dr Barrie Wade,
 Dr Hilary Minns
Series Designer: Jonathan Hair

Printed in China

Franklin Watts is a division of
Hachette Children's Books,
an Hachette UK company
www.hachette.co.uk

There is a puzzle at the end of this book.
Here are the answers for you to check later!

The matching words are:
Vic lick, pick, thick
fish dish, wish
chip dip, lip, ship, tip
Mog dog, fog, log

Vic is at the
fish and chip shop.

"Fish and chips, Kevin."

Kevin gets Vic a pack
of fish and chips.

Vic tucks the pack
in his jacket.

7

He sits in his van and has a long nap.

Mog gets Vic's fish and chips. She has the lot!

Vic gets a shock!

13

He has to go back to the fish and chip shop.

"Mog got the fish and chips. She had the lot!" Vic tells Kevin and Val.

Kevin tells Mog off.

Kevin gets Vic a big
pack of fish and chips.

18

Vic sits in the shop and has his fish and chips. He has the lot!

Puzzle Time!

Match the words that rhyme
to the pictures!

Vic

dish

log

dip

pick

fish

dog

lip

chip

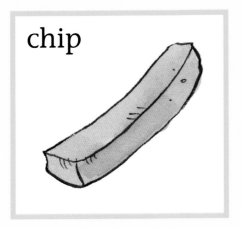

wish

tip

lick

ship

thick

fog

Mog

See page 2 for answers!

Notes for parents and teachers

READING CORNER PHONICS has been structured to provide maximum support for children learning to read through synthetic phonics. The stories are designed for independent reading but may also be used by adults for sharing with young children.

The teaching of early reading through synthetic phonics focuses on the 44 sounds in the English language, and how these sounds correspond to their written form in the 26 letters of the alphabet. Carefully controlled vocabulary makes these books accessible for children at different stages of phonics teaching, progressing from simple CVC (consonant-vowel-consonant) words such as "top" (t-o-p) to trisyllabic words such as "messenger" (mess-en-ger). READING CORNER PHONICS allows children to read words in context, and also provides visual clues and repetition to further support their reading. These books will help develop the all important confidence in the new reader, and encourage a love of reading that will last a lifetime!

If you are reading this book with a child, here are a few tips:

1. Talk about the story before you start reading. Look at the cover and the title. What might the story be about? Why might the child like it?

2. Encourage the child to reread the story, and to retell the story in their own words, using the illustrations to remind them what has happened.

3. Discuss the story and see if the child can relate it to their own experience, or perhaps compare it to another story they know.

4. Give praise! Small mistakes need not always be corrected. If a child is stuck on a word, ask them to try and sound it out and then blend it together again, or model this yourself. For example "wish" w-i-sh "wish".

READING CORNER PHONICS covers two grades of synthetic phonics teaching, with three levels at each grade. Each level has a certain number of words per story, indicated by the number of bars on the spine of the book:

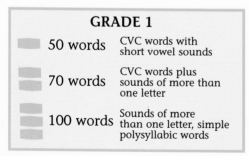

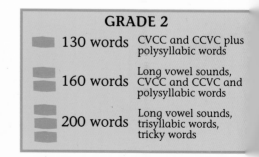

GRADE 1		GRADE 2	
50 words	CVC words with short vowel sounds	130 words	CVCC and CCVC plus polysyllabic words
70 words	CVC words plus sounds of more than one letter	160 words	Long vowel sounds, CVCC and CCVC and polysyllabic words
100 words	Sounds of more than one letter, simple polysyllabic words	200 words	Long vowel sounds, trisyllabic words, tricky words